Rome Wasn't
Burned in a Day

Rome Wasn't Burned in a Day:

THE MISCHIEF OF LANGUAGE

by
Leo Rosten

Illustrated by Rob't Day

Doubleday & Company, Inc.
Garden City, New York
1972

Library of Congress Catalog Card Number 72–132511
Copyright © 1972 by Leo Rosten
Illustrations Copyright © 1972 by Robert Day
All Rights Reserved
Printed in the United States of America

9   8   7   6   5   4   3   2

TO MY FRIENDS,
WHEREVER HE IS

CONTENTS

AUTHOR'S FOREWORD

THE MISCHIEF OF LANGUAGE

"Laughter," wrote Immanuel Kant, who was hardly a Falstaff, "is the sudden transformation of a tense expectation into nothing." Why Kant did not stop with "expectation," omitting "into nothing," I cannot understand.

This booklet is a medley of English sentences each of which, through the delicious imprecision of a word or the innocent refurbishing of a phrase, becomes a sudden transformation of an untense expectation into *something* —something startling or funny or illuminating or instructive. The most triumphant specimens are startling *and* funny and illuminating and instructive. Many of the bloopers are malapropisms; some are "Irish bulls"; others are farcical boners; but most are simply inspired departures from the familiar.

A malaprop, according to the Fowlers' *The King's English* ("—and so is the Queen!" cried Dizzy Dean), is a word used "in the belief that it has the meaning really belonging to another word that resembles it." Most malaprops are as dreary as that definition. The ones that most delight us are those that convert a platitude into a laugh ("A rolling stone gathers no moths"), or that titillate the mind with a revelation that has been lying around for centuries, waiting to be uttered ("Rome is full of fallen arches"), or that transform a cliché into an epigram—an inadvertent, unintended epigram, to be sure, but an aphorism nonetheless: pointed, memorable, a crisp distillation of a larger truth: "An oral contract isn't worth the paper it's written on."

Hobbes brilliantly described "the passion of laughter" as "sudden glory arising from sudden conception of some eminence in ourselves by comparison with the inferiority of others." This lovely insight explains why we feel superior, no less than amused, when we read such marvelous blunders as "Radium was discovered by Madman Curry," or "Underneath those shabby trousers beats a heart of gold." Each is a sudden, risible occasion for vainglory.

The cave men (whose descendants the theologians treat as fallen angels, and the Darwinians as ascended apes) probably laughed their heads off when a baboon slipped on a banana peel. It took centuries, I presume, before some *homo sapiens* reached the cerebral sophistication required to place a coconut where some sap would be sure to be conked by it.

The practical joker must have been the earliest wit in human history—and remains the most enduring: He is found in every primitive society, anthropologists tell me, as well as in Switzerland. I say Switzerland not because I am anti-Swiss but because, after a week in Zurich, I came to the conclusion that anything that can get a laugh in the yodel belt will tickle the ribs of men anywhere else.

12

It is my guess that our ancestors first laughed at a pratfall; later, laughter accompanied a practical joke ("monkey business"); later still, snickers followed some mistaken grunt of "Blgh" instead of "Ugh." Men fell on their butts long before they burbled a boo-boo, because you must *have* a word and know it and have it understood by your peers before its misuse will trigger a giggle.

The treasury of vocal bobbles is enriched each hour each day in every land on earth. Was there ever a child who did *not* come a cropper with a word? When my daughter was eight, she described something she had seen "as I was towardsing home"; when she was ten, she told a story that ended flatly: "This is my virgin of what happened"; when she was eleven, she sighed morosely, "I am a middle-aged child."

In a Winnetka kindergarten, some years ago, one lad drew a man with tiny, tailed creatures creeping all over him. When the foolish teacher asked what the drawing meant, young Raphael explained: "That's John, with all the mice on him." What John? What mice? "From the *pome:* 'Diddle, diddle dumpling, mice on John.'" I can find no way of faulting such peerless imagery. Or that of the tot who sang, "London britches falling down . . ." These delightful inventions are not, of course, in the same immortal league as that of the child who uttered a line that has surely been savored ten thousand times: "The equator is a menagerie lion who runs around the middle of the earth."

Given the ancient lineage and unceasing production of verbal goofs, it strikes me as astonishing that we had no name for the malaprop until the seventeenth century. I say the seventeenth century even though the word "malapropism" is usually associated with Mrs. Malaprop, a character in Sheridan's *The Rivals*, first performed in 1775. It turns out that Dryden preceded Sheridan by a century, when he enlisted a French phrase, *mal à propos*, to describe some false use of a word. But *mal à propos* happens to be quite inexact: it means improper, unseasonable, not pertinent—none of which is precisely what a malapropism is.

The length of time it took English writers and linguists to devise *some* name for amusing verbal fluffs is all the more striking if we consider how large is the supply of Greek or Latin roots available for English neologisms— itself a good example of wordbuilding (1803). Consider the array of technical terms we do use when we want to name, not describe, other forms of language play or ploy: oxymoron, metathesis, litotes, synecdoche, polyopton, mimesis, paronomasia, metonymy. They look outlandish, but they are exact and authoritative.*

Malapropists galore surely flourished in England and America long before Mrs. Malaprop, the matron saint of word manglers, appeared on the scene.† The pun was always a thigh slapper ("pun," by the way, is a Drydenian latecomer to English, too). The Elizabethans yakked their heads off over verbal incongruities. Shakespeare created word bumblers like Dogberry, Mistress Quickly,

---

* A more accurate word than "malapropism" would be "comicologism," or even "lapsus comicus," both coined for me, under duress, by Felix Kaufmann. They may be visually forbidding, but are they more brutal than the beauts above?

† One Heinz Stallman has produced a learned dissertation, *Malapropismen im englischen Drama von den Anfängen bis 1800* (Berlin: 1938), which lists a bibliography of fifteen titles.

14

Bottom, the Gravedigger in *Hamlet*.‡ Fielding named one of his characters Mrs. Slipslop, to emphasize her bungling of our pliant tongue.

Ireland's writers, all survivors of the Irish bull ("Ireland is overrun by absentee landlords"), have long employed jocular word jugglery, from Wilde to Joyce to O'Casey ("The world is in a state of chassis").

Englishmen, incidentally, have been patsies for a pun since the day a Londoner threw a sandwich at a pub mirror with the blasé quip "Is that not food for reflection?" But American humorists long seemed to prefer antic spelling as a lever of laughter. Linguistic crotchets are as old as American journalism; Josh Billings, Artemus Ward, Mark Twain, "Kin" Hubbard took impudent liberties with England's prose. And spiritual sisters to Mrs. Malaprop enlivened American letters in the form of Mrs. Partington, the brain child of one B. P. Shillaber, and Mrs. Spriggins, a *faux pas* female sired by John Bangs in the old comic magazine *Life*.** *1066 and All That*, by W. C. Sellar and R. J. Yeatman, was a 1930s carnival of historical and verbal doozies. The tradition has been carried on nobly by Richard Armour.

Ring Lardner was a genius at depicting idiots through their idiom (*You Know Me, Al*) and raked fools, scoundrels and sharpies with murderous parody ("Although he was not a good fielder, he was not a good hitter, either") or exquisite genteelisms ("Shut up," he explained).

‡ Bergen Evans, to whom I sent these observations, maintains that malapropisms might more properly be called "quicklyisms." ** See Evan Esar, *Humorous English* (Horizon Press, New York, 1961), *passim*.

William Faulkner used dialect with contrapuntal power; James Thurber, Anita Loos and Dorothy Parker deployed solecisms to deadly effect. S. J. Perelman is both an incomparable punster and a wizard of verbal miscegenation. Arthur Kober pinpointed the argot of the bygone Bronx for history (*Dear Bella*). And I daresay that H*Y*M*A*N K*A*P*L*A*N committed enough malapropian misdemeanors to keep the *mavens* at Oxford busy for a generation.

I often wonder why we do not hear, or hear of, far more bloomers and bloopers, considering the endless opportunities that present themselves in a language so rich in words, metaphors, similes and slang—all begging to be bowdlerized. Verbal mischief is ever latent and omnitempting in the English tongue.

"If crockery is a collection of crocks, then flattery is a collection of flats, scullery is a collection of skulls, sorcery a collection of sources, and monastery a collection of monsters. . . . (And) if jewelry is a collection of jewels, then husbandry is a collection of husbands, infantry is a collection of infants, vestry a collection of vests, and pantry a collection of pants. . . ."††

Or consider the realm of print, a veritable paradise for the all-thumbed. Recently, in checking the printers' galleys of an article I had written, I read, with utter astonishment: "The rapists tell us . . ." I placed an ice pack on my head after I realized that "the rapists" was

†† *Ibid*, pp. 69–70.

16

some Freudian typesetter's spatial improvement upon "therapists."

This kind of malaprintism, to coin a word, is the unending nightmare of editors and the recurring delight of readers. American folklore has sanctified the newspaper that referred to "Patrick Clancy, a defective on the police force," and hastily changed it in the next edition to: "Patrick Clancy is a detective on the police farce."

Sports-page editors learned from ghastly experience never, never to let the phrase "Babe Ruth's hits" get past them. . . . The cherubic perversity of printers has produced more than one obituary that announced that someone "did eat his home last night," or that some king, president or mayor was overtired because of "his official cuties." These katzenjammers are of another order from such transmutations of logic as have plagued the Chicago *Tribune* ("He got up, dressed and took a shower") or the New York *Times* ("He clung to the sill by his fingerprints. . . .").‡‡

"Typos," as typographical hanky-panky is called, seem to prove the validity of what some unknown sage has defined as Murphy's Law: "If something can go wrong, it will." In the reign of unhappy Charles I, the so-called "Wicked Bible" appeared, an unforgettable edition of Holy Scripture in which an errant (or diabolic) printer rendered the Seventh Commandment as: "Thou shalt commit adultery."

As the Van Buren (Arkansas) *Press-Argus* ruefully

‡‡ For all of these gems, I am grateful to Earle Tempel's *Press Boners* (Pocket Books, New York, 1967).

observed, centuries later, "It's nearly as hard to correct a typographical error as it is to get a woman unpregnant."*

But deeper, darker things are involved here. We have learned from Sigmund Freud that typos and slips of the tongue, malaprops and misnomers are not entirely innocent or accidental: Man's mistakes, no less than his dreams, are packed with meaning. *The Interpretation of Dreams* and *Wit and the Unconscious* are treasuries of dazzling revelations about comic errors that are, in fact, not errors but stratagems to evade the censors of the self.

Comedy is a complex masquerade—for anxiety, hostility, ambivalence or the unconscious need to diminish guilt by making light of what is taboo. Murder oft peeps through the masks of our wit. The corniest joke may convey feelings we are afraid to confront and reluctant to acknowledge, but do express from behind the protective visors of jest. And just as "free association" is never free, but is governed and guided by emotions ordinarily repressed, so humor is the unwitting messenger of truths that churn behind the camouflage of levity. There is method in our boners as well as our madness.

But what am I *say*ing? Not a smidgeon of psychoanalysis lurks in the pages that follow.

I have been collecting linguistic gewgaws ever since I wore knickers. In Hollywood, where I was indentured for a decade, no week passed unbrightened by some sparkling muff from one or another producer, director

* *Ibid.*

or actor. The moviemakers from Mittel-Europa were especially fecund joy givers to screenwriters: One Budapestian impresario solemnly invited me to cook up a story that would contain "a generous dearth of heart-robs about a great feedle player—someone like Sascha Heifetz."

Every so often I have included in this chrestomathy (don't turn pale; a chrestomathy is only a fancy name for a collection of literary goodies) a line that struck me as very funny, even though it was not, strictly speaking, a malaprop; why speak strictly at a time like this? Back in 1887 a testimonial advertisement featured an unshaved hobo saying, "I used your soap two years ago and have not used another since then." I do not think we should allow that to be lost in the humorless abysses of the past. I also dream of the day when some far-sighted foundation will establish a museum for menus, store signs, theater marquees and church plaques that clearly deserve immortality:

TODAY'S SPECIAL
Barely Soup

or

GOOD CLEAN DANCING
EVERY NIGHT
EXCEPT SUNDAY

or

Now Playing:
ADAM AND EVE
with a cast of thousands!

or

Today's Sermon:
HOW MUCH CAN A MAN DRINK?
*with hymns from
a full choir*

I have also included occasional corkers of the type
Thurber once classified as "Trivia Mundi, the younger
sister of Gloria."

It pains me to have found no way of including such
nifties as "Keeping a secret from him is like trying to
sneak the dawn past a rooster" (Fred Allen), "No man
ever forgets where he buried a hatchet" (Kin Hubbard),
"She's beautiful, an angel—with spurs" (Joe Pasternak),
"He looks like a dishonest Abe Lincoln" (of Harold Ross),
"You certainly have a ready wit; let me know when it's
ready" (Henny Youngman), or "You couldn't tell if she
was dressed for an opera or an operation" (Irvin S.
Cobb).

Wherever possible, I have credited a howler to the
source from which I obtained it (see Appendix). This
was not as simple as it sounds. I hear countless jokes,
wisecracks and spoonerisms bandied about by friends; God
only knows who originated them (the jokes, not the

friends—although I sometimes wonder about them, too). The actual origin of a funny anecdote, a pun, a snapper, a retort is often hopelessly entangled in the chain of conversational communications. It is just inevitable that the whoppers of one man will be attributed to another.

This is especially true in the case of a virtuoso like Mr. Samuel Goldwyn, whose gallery of malaprops has constantly been enlarged by cacologies which originated elsewhere. I have more than once heard an ad lib at the Brown Derby, say, or Sardi's, and read it in a gossip column the next day as having been coined by Mr. Goldwyn. I even have heretical doubts that that esteemed neologist actually coined the deathless "In two words: umpossible!" I say this because Jock Lawrence, then Mr. Goldwyn's press agent, used to beg many of us for *gaffes* he would then pass on to the Hollywood press— as 24-karat Goldwynisms.

I learned long ago not to be surprised by popular but incorrect attributions. After all, such historic utterances as "Go west, young man," "We have nothing to fear but fear itself," ". . . the iron curtain," "Ask not what your country can do for you; ask what you can do for your country" were *not* originated by (respectively) Horace Greeley, Franklin D. Roosevelt, Winston Churchill, John F. Kennedy.† The familiar "Any man who hates dogs and babies can't be all bad" is usually credited to W. C. Fields; but the line was uttered not by him but *about* him, by a young speaker at a Masquers' club dinner in

† See my "Well, I'll be Damned!" in *Look*, February, 10, 1970, p. 16.

the great man's honor: I ought to know; I was there.‡

Or again: I always thought it was in a debate in the House of Commons that Gladstone, stung beyond endurance by Disraeli's barbs, cried, "You, sir, will die either on the gallows or of some loathsome disease!"—only to hear Disraeli retort, "That, sir, depends upon whether I embrace your principles or your mistress." Only yesterday (and I *do* mean yesterday) did I learn that the incomparable exchange took place in the eighteenth century, between the Earl of Sandwich and John Wilkes, a libertine of exceptional agility.

I have no doubt that one or another professional jokesmith will bleat that one or another line in this lexicon is "really" his. I can only reply that if I heard it from him, or heard it attributed to him, or read it in anything he created, or had not found it in a reputable source that clearly predated the alleged invention, I have, Scout's honor, gladly identified him as the father or mother of the child. As Ruskin beautifully declaimed, "Masked words (are always) droning and skulking about us."

One final *caveat:* Never underestimate the ancestry of a squib. "Athens is a great place to visit, but I wouldn't want to live there" sounds as contemporary as bubble gum, but that put-down was tossed off by Isocrates, a ghost-writer of the fourth century B.C. You would be startled by the number of current japeries that can be traced back to Epictetus, Marcus Aurelius, Gracián, Erasmus, Montaigne, Francis Bacon, Voltaire, Samuel

‡ See Rhoda Thomas Tripp, *International Thesaurus of Quotations,* (Crowell, New York, 1970), p. 406.

Johnson, La Rochefoucauld, Whistler, G. K. Chesterton, Wilde, Mark Twain, Bernard Shaw, Stephen Leacock, Wilson Mizner, George S. Kaufman, *et,* as they say, *cetera.*

As a seasoned tautologist would put it: Some things are so unexpected that no one is prepared for them.

—*Leo Rosten*

October 18, 1971
New York, New York

I • ADAGES DOWN THE AGES

"Give a man enough rope and he'll hang you."[1]

❀

"A rolling stone gathers no moths."[2]

❀

"Don't blame God—he's only human."[3]

❀

"Beware of a Greek who asks for a gift."[4]

❀

"Don't bite the hand that lays the golden egg."[5]

❀

"Barking dogs don't bite people they don't know."[6]

✻

"Don't burn your bridges till you come to them."[7]

✿

"Don't put all your chickens in one basket."[8]

✿

"Every silver lining has a cloud around it."[9]

✿

"He who laughs last, lasts."[10]

✿

"In the kingdom of the one-eyed, he would steal you blind."[11]

✿

"He is only as honest as the day is long."[12]

*

"Let's get down to brass roots."[13]

❀

"Let sleeping ducks lie."[14]

❀

"Many are cold but few are frozen."[15]

❀

"Money roots out all evil."[16]

❀

"Never let a gift horse in the house."[17]

❀

"Hear today, deaf tomorrow."[18]

✿

"None but the brave desert the fair."[19]

❊

"People who live in glass houses shouldn't get stoned."[20]

❊

"The wish is farther than the thought."[21]

❊

"When we come to that bridge, we'll jump off it."[22]

❊

"You better go through this with a fine tooth and a comb."[23]

❊

32

"Rome wasn't burned in a day."[24]

✿

33

"Where there's a will, there's a wail."[25]

✿

"You have to take the bad with the worst."[26]

❋

II • ADVICE

"Never undress in front of a bearded lady."[27]

✿

"Don't let a crack like that bother you; let it roll off your back like a duck."[28]

✿

"Don't be a pessimist, always building dungeons in the air."[29]

✿

"Don't pay attention to him; don't even ignore him!"[30]

✿

"Remember that when it comes to giving, some people stop at nothing."[31]

✿

"You can observe a lot by watching."[32]

✾

"If your eye falls on a bargain, pick it up."[33]

❁

III • ALLUSIONS AND METAPHORS

"He's just a wolf in cheap clothing."[34]

✿

"In Tel Aviv, I led the life of Levy."[35]

✿

"No one's perfect; everyone has his chilly heel."[36]

✿

"That's like carrying Cohens to New Rochelle."[37]

✿

"He's had so many romances he's a regular Don
Coyote."[38]

✢

IV • ANIMAL LORE

"A centimeter shows how far a centipede crawls."[39]

✿

"Achilles beat the tortoise by a hair."[40]

✿

"A leopard is a form of dotted lion."[41]

✿

"Anteaters are generally found at picnics."[42]

✿

"Dogs are getting bigger, according to a leading dog manufacturer."[43]

✿

"Female moths are called myths."[44]

✻

"He was an engaging little dog, said an observer with a curly tail and friendly manner."[45]

✻

"Miss O'Hayer has been raising birds for many years and is credited with having the largest parateets in the state."[46]

✻

"Pheasants were treated something terrible in the Middle Ages."[47]

✻

"The cotton crop was ruined by bold weasels."[48]

✻

"Quails are generally afraid of something."[49]

❀

V • THE ARTS

"Lola Carlisle, a budding author, said that she had circulated her navel unsuccessfully among various Hollywood producers."[50]

BALLET

"If I was in this business for the business, I wouldn't be in business."[51]

✿

LITERATURE

"That book was so exciting I couldn't finish it until I put it down!"[52]

✿

"How would you like to write my autobiography?"[53]

✿

"He's such a good writer, he won the Pullet Surprise."[54]

✿

"He doesn't waste a word; everything he writes is full of pith."[55]

✿

50

MOVIES

"The most important thing in acting is *honesty;* once you learn to fake that, you're in!"[56]

❀

"What do you mean it's too caustic? Who cares about expense?"[57]

❀

"This story is wonderful. It's magnificent. It's prolific!"[58]

❀

"The wide screen makes bad movies twice as bad."[59]

❀

"The scene is dull; tell him to put more life into his dying."[60]

❀

51

"She's not vulgar; in fact, she's couth."[61]

❀

"This book has too much plot and not enough story."[62]

❁

"She's got talent and personality. Give me two years, and I'll make her an overnight star."[63]

❁

"Can we change the heroine from a lesbian to an American?"[64]

❁

"A producer shouldn't get ulcers; he should give them."[65]

❁

MUSIC

"They sang like angels; no instruments, just Acapulco."[66]

❁

53

"Early in his career, he switched from the guitar to the mandarin."[67]

✿

THEATER

(Director to actors): "Please stand a little closer apart."[68]

✿

"It's a terrible play: Don't fail to miss it if you can."[69]

✿

"Go see it and see for yourself why you shouldn't go see it."[70]

✿

VI • BONERS

(from a free press)

"There are millions of desirable women who are unattacked and hungry for love."[71]

❁

"The doctor felt the man's purse and said there was no hope."[72]

❁

"There was something about that title, Old Incestors' Trading Corporation, that inspired confidence."[73]

❁

"He heard himself assailed as a self-centered financial executive who buttered his own beard."[74]

❁

"Picking up his hammer, nails and two broads, he went back into the cabin to finish the job."[75]

❁

VII • BUSINESS

Insights and Stratagems

"Excuse me for not answering your
letter sooner, but I've been so
busy not answering letters that I
couldn't get around to not answering
yours in time."[76]

"I go to the bank whenever I want to ransack that type of business."[77]

❋

"Businessmen talk about business the way they talk about sex: When it's good, it's very, *very* good; and when it's bad, it's not so bad."[78]

❋

"I'd give my right arm to have that man as my right hand."[79]

❋

"Horace Greeley knew the answer: 'Wear a vest, young man, wear a vest!'"[80]

❋

"At least half their customers who fly to
New York come by plane."[81]

✺

59

"That guy robs me the wrong way."[82]

*

VIII • CAROLS, HYMNS, PLEDGES AND RHYMES

(as gathered from a covey of children)

"God rest ye, Jerry Mandelbaum. . . ."[83]

Pledge of Allegiance

"I pledge allegiance to the flag and to the republic for Richard Stands; one naked individual, with liberty's injustice for all."[84]

✿

The Lord's Prayer

"Our Father, who art in heaven, Halloween thy name. Thy kingdom come, thy will be done on earth as it is in heaven. Give us this day our daily bread. And forgive us our press passes, as we forgive those who press past us. And lead us not into Penn Station, but deliver us from Emil. For thine is the kingdom, and the powder, and the glory, forever. A man."[85]

✿

God Bless America

"God bless America,
Land that I love,
Stand aside her
And guy her,
With delight
Through the night
From a bulb."[86]

✿

Gladly, the Cross I Bear . . .

"Gladly, the cross-eyed bear . . ."[87]

❁

Diddle, Diddle, Dumpling

"Diddle, diddle, dumpling
Mice on John
One shoe off and one shoe on."[88]

❁

London Bridge

"London britches falling down,
Falling town, falling town."[89]

❁

Hark! the Herald Angels

"Hark, the angel Harold sings,
Glory to the new brown King. . . ."[90]

❁

63

IX • A CATALOGUE OF CHARACTERS

"He's the type who'll cut your throat behind your back."[91]

❀

"The most unpleasant thing about him is that when he isn't drunk, he's sober."[92]

❀

"Every time he opens his mouth he puts his foot in the soup."[93]

❀

"He's got the kind of face that looks as though he's already been waited on."[94]

❀

"He's such an insomniac that when he's asleep
he dreams he's not sleeping."[95]

✿

X • CHILDREN
—and parents

"Be careful, Johnny; if you hurt yourself, I'll kill you!"[96]

✿

"If your father was alive, he'd be turning over in his grave."[97]

✿

"Mother no's best."[98]

✿

XI • COME AGAIN?

"While he may be poor and shabby,
underneath those ragged trousers
beats a heart of gold."[99]

❀

"A stray bullet killed one bystander slightly."[100]

✿

"The ball struck him on the right temple and knocked him cold. He was taken to Ford Hospital where X rays of his head showed nothing."[101]

✿

"He ran his hand through his hair and pulled out a cigar."[102]

✿

"He gave her a diamond that sparkled at every faucet."[103]

✿

"He and his wife left Sunday for Florida, and we all hope they will like their trip and stay in Miami."[104]

✿

"A lot of people my age are dead at the
present time."[105]

❋

73

"Push back the cuticle with the orange stick
dipped in liquid cuticle remover.
While you do one hand, soak the other."[107]

75

"My wife's hands are so beautiful, I'm having
a bust made of them."[108]

*

"He sent the package by partial post."[109]

✿

"The difference between a fort and a fortress is that if it has breastworks, it's a fortress."[110]

✿

XII • CRISES

"The flood damage was so bad they had to evaporate four cities."[111]

❀

"The police surrounded the building on three sides and threw an accordion around the block."[112]

❀

"The Fire Department will blow the siren fifteen minutes before the start of each fire."[113]

❀

Emergency message from boat to deep-sea diver: "Come up fast! The ship is sinking!"[114]

❀

"The bride was wearing an old lace gown that fell
to the floor as she came down the aisle."[115]

❀

XIII • DECORUM

"Hi! It's been a long time since I haven't seen you."[116]

✿

"I don't want a single thing left undone that might cause the slightest inconvenience to my guests."[117]

✿

"His mind may be slow, but it's *dull*."[118]

✿

"We wish to thank our many friends and neighbors for their kind assistance in the recent destruction of our home by fire."[119]

✿

"I don't want to join the kind of club that accepts people like me as members."[120]

✿

84

"So long—and say hello to anybody."[121]

✲

"When you talk to me, shut up."[122]

✿

"I just want to thank everyone who made this day necessary."[123]

✿

XIV • EDUCATION

"Latin is the language of the dead."[124]

✿

"He's *very* smart. He has an I.Q."[125]

✿

"You can observe a lot by watching."[126]

✿

"He is a student in the Episcopal seminary at Cambridge, which is afflicted with Harvard University."[127]

✿

"For your information, just answer me one
question."[128]

*

XV • THE FAMILY OF MAN

"The English call a rest room a Waterloo."[129]

✿

"Filipinos do wonders with baboon furniture."[130]

✿

"The French national anthem is the
Mayonnaise."[131]

✿

"Italics is the language the Italians write in."[132]

✿

"Jews are like everyone else, only more so."[133]

✿

"Mohammedans wear a fuzz, but Hindus prefer turbines."[134]

❀

"You always have to keep a watch on the Swiss."[135]

❀

Hungarian cookbook recipe for an omelette: "First, steal two eggs . . ."[136]

❀

XVI • FAMOUS PEOPLE

EDGAR ALLAN POE

"Achilles' mother held him by the heel and dipped him in a stinking river."[137]

✿

"Beethoven had ten children and practiced on a spinster in the attic."[138]

✿

"The author of Aesop's Fables was Aesophagus."[139]

✿

"Radium was discovered by Madman Curry."[140]

✿

"The Gorgons looked like women, only more horrible."[141]

✿

"Our first president was Judge Washington. Then came Tom S. Jefferson. Then came James Medicine. But the best was Abraham Lincohen."[142]

❖

"The most famous of all Italian composers is Libretto."[143]

❁

"The Parthenon was the she-wolf who nursed Romeo in Joliet."[144]

❁

"The bravest of all Indian scouts was Daniel Bloom."[145]

❁

"The two worst traitors in American history were Ben and Dick Arnold."[146]

❁

"*The Clouds* was written by the ancient Greek playwright Mephistopheles."[147]

❁

"Washington's farewell address was Mount Vernon."[148]

✿

"The law of gravity was discovered by Isaac Newman."[149]

✿

XVII • GEOGRAPHY

"Alcazar is what you take for an upset stomach."[150]

✿

"Pompeii was once completely buried in larva."[151]

✿

"The Pyramids are a rocky range of mountains between France and Spain."[152]

✿

"It's a really beautiful spot where the hand of man has never set foot."[153]

✿

"Parts of the Grand Canyon are a mile deep and two miles high."[154]

"Rome is full of fallen arches."[155]

✿

"Dear Folks: Next, we will drive to Gnome,
Alaska. . . ."[156]

❋

XVIII • GOD'S DOMAIN

"It's the age-old story: God versus Satin."[158]

❈

"The three Magis were named Frank, Incense and Mur."[159]

❈

"Infidels are not Christians: They practice infidelity."[160]

❈

"The first thing they do when a baby is born is cut its biblical cord."[161]

❈

"Joshua won the battle of Geritol."[162]

❈

"Noah's wife was Joan of Ark."[163]

❁

"They should lock up all those monsters in a monastery."[164]

❁

"Reverend Hammond was congratulated on being able to get his parish plastered."[165]

❁

XIX • THE GOOD LIFE

"*No* one ever goes to that restaurant any more; it's too crowded!"[166]

✿

"This week, the Saturday matinee will be held on Tuesday instead of Thursday."[167]

✿

"My favorite waltz is the Blue Daniel."[168]

✿

"These shoes? I only use them for streetwalking."[169]

✿

"Ever since he retired, he does nothing but play
Jim Rummy."[170]

❋

"Rich? He's a malted millionaire!"[171]

XX • A HANDFUL OF HISTORY

"When you mean longer ago than 'then,' you say 'thence.'"[172]

✿

"No humans were around in those days because it was the preastork age."[173]

✿

"The Bible describes how Samson fought the Finkelsteins."[174]

✿

"Ancient Egypt was inhabited by mummies, and they all wrote in hydraulics."[175]

✿

"During that mania, they burned every witch in Witchita."[176]

✿

116

"The capital of China once was Dresden."[177]

❂

"She is like Caesar's wife—all things to all men."[178]

❂

XXI • HEARTH AND HOME

"Did you wash and wrench the dishes?"[179]

Note in bottle: "Please leave 2 qts. of homicide milk."[180]

❁

"She was in the kitchen putting on the water for a few sandwiches."[181]

❁

"I never knew it would cost so much to landscape my house."[182]

❁

"By the time he had the bird in hand he was
bushed."[183]

XXII • THE KING'S ENGLISH

COMCHIEF
FLEET H.Q.

FOG IMPENETRABLE. SHALL I PROCEED   OR
RETURN TO BASE?
                    S.S. COLFAX

S.S. COLFAX
            YES.
                    COMCHIEF

COMCHIEF

DO YOU MEAN PROCEED OR RETURN?
                    S.S. COLFAX

S.S. COLFAX
            NO.
                    COMCHIEF[184]

✿

"Man, did he make a wrong mistake!"[185]

❀

"In two words: Umpossible."[186]

❀

"The principal parts of the verb 'to fail' are: fail, failed, bankrupt."[187]

❀

"Past tense means you used to be nervous."[188]

❀

"Do you have a nice double room where I can put up with my wife?"[189]

❀

"I know the King's English—and so is the Queen."[190]

✿

XXIII • LAW

"He was sent to prison for strangling a woman without killing her."[191]

❀

"A verbal contract isn't worth the paper it's written on."[192]

❀

"That crime gets an automatic penalty of twenty years in Alabama."[193]

❀

"Before the court sentenced him, the defendant was asked if he had anything to say. In a calm voice, and without the least sign of emotion, he said nothing."[194]

❀

"The jury's verdict showed they were of one mind:
temporarily insane."[195]

✿

"The kindly rain doth fall upon
The just and unjust fellow,
But mostly on the just
Because
The unjust stole the just's
umbrella."[196]

XXIV • LIFE AND DEATH

"He was such a hypochondriac that they buried
him next to a doctor."[197]

"Life is a tale told by an idiot, full of funny sounds and phooey."[198]

❂

"The principle parts of 'to die' are: die, dead, funeral."[199]

❂

At a movie producer's huge funeral:
"It only goes to show what happens when you give the public what it wants."[200]

❂

"He wants to be cremated because he doesn't believe in death."[201]

❂

XXV • LOGIC

"He went to jail for making a false deduction."[202]

✿

"You fail to overlook the crucial point."[203]

✿

"The driver swerved to avoid missing the woman's husband."[204]

✿

"I get up six o'clock in the morning no
matter what time it is."[205]

✻

XXVI • MALE AND FEMALE

"A girl who is seventeen is much more of a woman than a boy who is seventeen."[206]

✲

"Women are the best other sex men have."[207]

✲

"Women tend to get all jumpy during their minstrel periods."[208]

✲

Letter of twelve-year-old boy to ten-year-old girl: "Your mother was murdered. Before she died, she told me to tell you *she doesn't want you to play in my yard any more!*"[209]

✲

"Women love him because he knows how far to go too far."[210]

✲

"Home is where you hang your head."[211]

✿

"Mr. Okum lives with his wife, his high school sweetheart, and three sons."[212]

✿

"My wife called me from London last night. It was wonderful to hear her voice and realize she was over three thousand miles away."[213]

✿

"No one heard him laugh like that since his wife died."[214]

✿

XXVII • MEDICINE

"He collapsed on the sidewalk and died without medical assistance."[215]

❁

"What should you do for hives?"
"Nothing. They are enemies."[216]

❁

"Miss Swanson is in the hospital this morning after having been bitten by a spider in a bathing suit."[217]

❁

"Antidotes are what you take to prevent dotes."[218]

❁

"The dentist had her in the chair two hours working on her morals."[219]

❁

"They would have given him artificial perspiration, but he voluntarily regained consciousness."[220]

✿

XXVIII • POLITICS

"Politics makes strange postmasters."[221]

✿

"Their father is some kind of civil serpent."[222]

✿

"I challenge my opponent to give a frank, affirmative answer: Yes or No!"[223]

✿

"Wherever the President goes, he's guarded by social security agents."[224]

✿

"The President of the United States must be an American citizen unless he was born here."[225]

✿

"And I promise you that if elected, I will be neither partial nor impartial."[226]

*

XXIX • PSYCHOLOGY

(of a sort)

"I've got mine trained so that every time I run
the maze in a certain way he has to feed me."[226A]

"A psychologist is a man who, when a beautiful girl walks into a room, watches other men's reaction."[227]

❀

"A kleptomaniac can't help helping himself."[228]

❀

"Put it out of your mind; in no time, it will be a forgotten memory."[229]

❀

"Any man who goes to a psychiatrist ought to have his head examined."[230]

XXX • RADIO BOO-BOOS

(all true)

"Do you wake up feeling tired and lustless?"[231]

❀

"In exactly thirty seconds it will be approximately 1:15."[232]

✿

"It strikes me as funny, don't you?"[233]

✿

"Suppose we reminisce a little about tomorrow's fight."[234]

✿

"After this announcement, we will continue with our uninterrupted music."[235]

✿

"You get just what you pay for, and you don't pay very much."[236]

✿

"For Christmas, why not give your wife a
gorgeous Gruen?"[237]
(Repeat, increasing tempo, until lightning strikes.)

❀

"And now—stay stewed for the nudes!"[238]

❋

XXXI • ROYALTY

"Since some queens can't marry kings,
they arrange to have concerts."[239]

"The king wore a velvet robe trimmed with beautiful white vermin."[240]

❀

"A duchy is the wife of a duke."[241]

❀

"The book is all about English royalty: castles, butlers, buttresses . . ."[242]

❀

XXXII • SCIENCE

"They better not fool around with that atomic bomb—it's dynamite!"[243]

❀

(On being told what a sun-dial is for): "My God! What'll they think of next?"[244]

❀

"Damp weather is very hard on the sciences."[245]

❀

"We now know that the moon is uninhibited."[246]

❀

"Through a telescope you can see the creators of the moon."[247]

❀

"The tides are named Eb and Flo."[248]

❋

"Flying saucers are just an optical conclusion."[249]

✿

XXXIII • THE SPORTING WORLD

"The baseball game continued in the cow pasture —and ended abruptly when a runner slid into what he thought was second base."[250]

❀

"You have to remember that this team came up slow, but *fast*."[251]

❀

"The Yankees, as I told you later, are in a slump."[252]

❀

"He loves to watch the boats sail pro and con."[253]

❀

"The grandstand was so crowded they had to turn down people for seats."[254]

XXXIV • O TEMPURA! O MORRIE!

"Ronald? What kind of a name is that? Today, every Tom, Dick and Harry is called Ronald."[255]

❋

"They have an old-fashioned house—two stories but no addict."[256]

❋

"The ancestors of the Daniel Burton family will meet on Sunday at Edgemont Park for their annual reunion."[257]

❋

"A good way to start any affair is by singing 'The
Star-Spangled Banner.'"[258]

XXXV • THE WEATHER

"And here is the weather forecast: Rain and slow, followed by sneet."[259]

❀

"It wasn't much of a rainfall, just a typical summer drivel."[260]

❀

"It's zero outside—no temperature at all."[261]

❀

"The weather forecast: Snow, followed by little boys with sleds."[262]

❀

REFERENCE NOTES,
CREDITS, DISCREDITS
AND QUANDARIES

1. Leo Rosten.

2. *Ibid.* (*Ibid.* is the abbreviated form of *ibidem*, a Latin adverb, highly prized and resolutely used by scholars; it actually means "in that very place," "just there," or even "moreover," but is generally used to indicate "the same reference as above.")

3. Leo Rosten, *A Trumpet for Reason,* Doubleday, New York, 1970, p. 68.

4. Leo Rosten.

5. Attributed to Samuel Goldwyn, the distinguished movie producer; but also credited to one or another candy manufacturer, clothing merchant, Hollywood mogul or habitué of Seventh Ave., which is a treasure house of malaprops.

6. Leo Rosten.

7. A famous American general whose name, though legendary, is not to be bandied about; reported to me by Ken McCormick. Let's credit this to General Legendary.

8. Leo Rosten.

9. *Ibid.*

10. *Ibid.*

11. *Ibid.* (Sorry if this is becoming tiresome.)

12. *Ibid.* (I blush.)

13. Reported by William Bernbach (whose first name is not Doyle Dane), who swears he heard it from an esteemed and sober client.

14. Leo Rosten (in whose youth, on the West Side of Chicago, the elders so often pronounced dogs "ducks" and ducks "docks" that it was hard to know whether a speaker was referring to a physician or a fowl).

15. *Ibid.*

16. *Ibid.*

17. *Ibid.* (I, as well as Ibid, heard this.)

18. *Ibid.*

19. Addison Mizner—and one of the finest puns I know.

20. I heard this at a Hollywood party.

21. Leo Rosten.

22. See note 7.

23. Leo Rosten.

24. Leo Rosten, *A Trumpet for Reason,* op. cit.

25. Leo Rosten, in "My Handy-Dandy Plan to Save Our Colleges," *Look* magazine, December 15, 1970, p. 81.

26. Jerome ("Dizzy") Dean, celebrated baseball pitcher and sports announcer, in a television program I heard with my own ears, not having anyone else's handy.

27. Evan Esar, *Humorous English,* Horizon Press, New York, 1961, p. 113.

28. Attributed to Samuel Goldwyn, but please note the noteworthy *caveat* under note 5.

29. My adaptation of some unwitty wit's effort to coin a witticism.

30. Reported to me by Daniel Bell, distinguished Harvard sociologist; Professor Bell, who has an encyclopedic command of things printed, is especially skillful in attributing sayings to the Talmud which exist only in the Talmud of his own mind.

31. A Yiddish proverb: Its verity can be validated by any fund-raiser for a worthy cause.

32. Lawrence ("Yogi") Berra, immortal catcher for the New York Yankees and a word juggler of salubrious originality; when he first became a baseball manager, forever doffing his face mask and chest protector, a skeptical reporter asked whether it would not be difficult to manage a ball club, after so many years of simply playing on one—to which Mr. Berra replied in this immortal comment on the learning process.

33. Leonard Q. Ross (Leo Rosten), *The Education of H*Y*M*A*N K*A*P*L*A*N,* Harcourt, Brace & Co., New York, p. 68. Mr. Kaplan regarded the English language pretty much the way a child treats Silly Putty.

34. Leo Rosten.

35. George Jessel, at a Bonds for Israel banquet, upon his return from the Promised Land. The trip was worth it if only for this observation.

36. One of Leo Rosten's children, unnamed here to protect him/her from the winces of his/her peers, if such indeed exist. You will also find a version of this in Art Linkletter's *Children Sure Rite Funny!*, Bernard Geis & Associates, Random House, New York, 1962.

37. Leo Rosten.

38. *Ibid;* I admit this one is pretty wild—but so was Oscar.

39. *Ibid,* though this no doubt has been said, at one time or another, by some chipper child in Lapatubbee Creek, Mississippi.

40. *Ibid.*—and a *faux pas* so obvious that I am astonished never to have run across it.

41. Leonard L. Levinson, *The Left Handed Dictionary,* Collier Books, New York, 1963, p. 126.

42. Adapted from Leonard L. Levinson, a whiz at funny one liners.

43. Duluth (Minn.) *News Tribune,* quoted by Earle Tempel, *Press Boners,* Pocket Books, New York, 1967.

44. Leonard L. Levinson, *op. cit.,* p. 153.

45. New Castle (N.Y.) *Tribune,* quoted by Earle Tempel, *Press Boners, op. cit.*

46. From the New York *Times,* culled by Earle Tempel, *More Press Boners,* Pocket Books, New York, 1968, p. 9.

47. Art Linkletter, *A Child's Garden of Misinformation,* Bernard Geis & Associates, Random House, New York, 1965. Mr. Linkletter's garden is a delight for foo-foo fanciers.

48. Leo Rosten, who is no horticulturist.

49. *Ibid,* who quails at the thought.

50. From the unhappy Chicago *Tribune,* as quoted by the cherubic Earle Tempel, *More Press Boners, op. cit.,* p. 160.

51. Mr. Sol Hurok, the world's most resourceful impresario, commenting on the staggering costs involved in importing 532 members of the Bolshoi Opera Company from Moscow, for their debut in our land. The project was canceled at the customary last moment by the Soviet Government for reasons that are not clear to anyone—including, I suspect, the Soviet

Government. When I asked a leading Kremlinologist to analyze the Cold War implications of the brusque rebuff, he thought carefully, tapped out his pipe and went to lunch.

52. Leo Rosten, adapted from Art Linkletter's *Kids Sure Rite Funny!*

53. From a letter to me by an alleged admirer (I had to read the line twice, too).

54. Art Linkletter, *Kids Sure Rite Funny!;* also used by Norton Mockridge, *Fractured English,* Doubleday, New York, 1965.

55. Leo Rosten, who didn't mean to make it a pun—or even an exact description.

56. The most incisive comment I ever heard about the art of acting, heard at a dinner table in Hollywood, where dinner tables crackle with crisp cracks and spontaneous aphorisms.

57. One or another movie producer; I have heard this one attributed to Gregory Ratoff, Samuel Goldwyn, Harry Cohn, and somebody's uncle—in the days when nepotism ran riot in Baghdad on the Pacific.

58. *This* one was coined in an outburst of enthusiasm by Mr. Goldwyn.

59. *Ibid.,* in an outburst of contempt—and foresight.

60. Attributed, *ad hoc,* to Messrs. Ratoff, Goldwyn, or Michael Curtiz, gifted movie director.

61. See note 57.

62. Samuel Goldwyn—and it remains a most acute observation on the paramount deficiency of melodrama as a literary form.

63. See note 57.

64. An old one, but immortal; attributed right and left, but most often to a Rumanian movie producer; see note 57.

65. Samuel Goldwyn, in a telephone conversation with Dore Schary, at that time chief of Metro-Goldwyn-Mayer studios. Mr. Schary recently was Commissioner of Cultural Affairs for the City of New York. This is not a *sequitur.*

177

66. Attributed to Joseph Pasternak, a movie producer not related to Boris.

67. This one has been hanging around for centuries, waiting to be uttered—by the author of this lexicon.

68. Attributed to Michael Curtiz, from Hungary, or Gregory Ratoff, from Russia. Neither of these talented men was from hunger.

69. Anyone raised in the Bronx, Brooklyn, Queens or Flatbush must have heard this a hundred times; it brightened my life only after I moved to New York and heard it from a native.

70. Faultless logic by Samuel Goldwyn, so they say, and who am I to gainsay them?

71. Omaha (Neb.) *Shopping Guide,* quoted by Earle Tempel, *Press Boners.*

72. Norton Mockridge, *op. cit.*

73. Earle Tempel, *Press Boners,* quoting an item in the New York *Journal American.*

74. Terre Haute (Ind.) *Tribune,* quoted by Earle Tempel, *More Press Boners.*

75. *Ibid.* (Our old friend.)

76. Julius ("Groucho") Marx, in a letter to me. Mr. Marx's lunar correspondence, which properly reposes in the archives of the Library of Congress, contains inimitable comments on American vaudeville, theater, movies and radio; the Marxian canon will greatly help those historians of the future it does not drive mad.

77. Leo Rosten, who will no doubt be challenged by a dozen jokesmiths, each claiming this one as his very own; I have no doubt that some high school English teacher read this, at one time or another, in a student's composition.

78. I heard this one over drinks with the late Beardsley Ruml; he tossed it off in his usual mordant manner; the *aperçu* has since been attributed to a gallimaufry of lesser characters.

178

79. Reported to me by William Bernbach, who often reports to me.

80. Leo Rosten, who is amazed no one said it before.

81. A contestant on one of Groucho Marx's television programs, "You Bet Your Life" said, "I flew here from Australia by plane." Joke writers have since used this line in other contests.

82. Leo Rosten—and I can prove it.

83. This priceless bowdlerization was reported in a "Talk of the Town" item in *The New Yorker,* years ago; I can't remember the year, I can't find the date, and I won't answer a single inquiry about it.

84. This is a compilation of various fruity boo-boos reported by Art Linkletter, Norton Mockridge, *The New Yorker,* and *Vayr Vayst,* who else.

85. *Ibid.*

86. *Ibid.*

87. This one is as old as the hills. (Mrs. Hill is ninety-six.)

88. Reported to me by Bergen Evans, as reported to him by a Winnetka school principal, as reported to him by a kindergarten teacher.

89. I have run across this in half a dozen places I am too lazy to list.

90. The first line is known to 3,460,592 mothers; the second line is mine. Mine, I tell you, *mine.*

91. An old canard, in various versions; this one was contributed by Bruno Schachner, New York counselor-at-law, authority on Emperor Franz Joseph, savings programs, and medieval laws anent mopery. (Mopery has nothing to do with moping; it has nothing to do with law, either; Mr. Schachner was miseducated in Vienna.)

92. Adapted from W. B. Yeats.

93. Leo Rosten.

94. Wally Cox, on an NBC television program.

95. Louis A. Safian, *2000 Insults for All Occasions,* Citadel Press, New York, 1965, a windfall for TV joke writers.

96. A Stamford (Conn.) mother, to her psychiatrist.

97. This one, which surfaces periodically, originated in a Yiddish saying that has been transmuted down the years.

98. Dorothy Parker.

99. The Boston *Globe,* quoted by Earle Tempel, *Press Boners,* p. 119.

100. Maryville (Mo.) *Forum,* quoted by Earle Tempel, *Press Boners.*

101. New York *Herald Tribune, Ibid.* The item referred to an accident suffered by Yogi Berra, who was hit on the head by a wild pitch, was rushed to a hospital, and subsequently told the palpitating press that the X rays of his head showed nothing.

102. I wish I could remember the source of this one; I *think* it was the encyclopedic Mr. Tempel, whose catalogue of malaprints is second to none's, as Peter de Vries' Mrs. Wallop would say.

103. From a child's composition. Gems like this give child's play a good name.

104. Marble Falls (Tex.) *Messenger,* as reported by Earle Tempel (who else?), *Press Boners.*

105. Charles Dillon ("Casey") Stengel, peerless baseball pundit, for a decade manager of the immortal New York Yankees. Grammarians who have studied Mr. Stengel's English are driven to the conclusion that he is as articulate as he appears confused; he simply uses free-wheeling syntax to communicate observations of the utmost originality. Whether Mr. Stengel befuddles himself as much as his listeners has never been ruled on authoritatively.

106. There was such a sign in a boardinghouse in the West, and I wish Mark Twain had seen it.

107. Hagerstown (Md.) *Herald,* quoted by Earle Tempel, *Press Boners.*

108. This genteelism goes back to the eighteenth century; it is constantly attributed to Samuel Goldwyn and to a New York candy manufacturer, who may also have said it. Like

180

the famous Darwin-Wallace coincidence, and the James-Lange theory, such things do happen independently, if only to remind us of the fallacy of *post hoc ergo propter hoc.* (If you put a post into hock, a prop man will replace it.)

109. Art Linkletter, *Kids Sure Rite Funny!* And they do.

110. I heard a Navy captain toss this off at a luncheon in Washington; whether it was original with him, I do not know, but I'll wager it has been claimed by many military *mayvonim.*

111. I would be greatly surprised if this isn't in one or another of Art Linkletter's charming collections of kiddies' English mishmash. I found it in the attic of my memory.

112. Art Linkletter, *Kids Sure Rite Funny!*

113. Ontario (N.Y.) *Wayne County Mail,* quoted by Tempel, *Press Boners.*

114. This discombobulating message will be found in Gerald F. Lieberman's debatably titled *The Greatest Laughs of All Time,* Curtis Books, Modern Literary Editions Publishing Company, 1961, p. 146.

115. Earle Tempel (bless his soul!), *More Press Boners.*

116. This stopper is recorded exactly the way I was greeted, by an acquaintance at the City Athletic Club; I have since heard that New Yorkers do not consider it novel. I think it a triumph of paralogy.

117. New York *Daily News,* as quoted by Tempel, *More Press Boners.*

118. Dorothy Parker, in my presence, during a stretch in Hollywood for committing movies; we were dining at Dave Chasen's restaurant, a favorite watering hole for screen writers.

119. Laramie (Wyo.) *Boomerang,* quoted by Tempel, *Press Boners,* p. 47.

120. Groucho Marx, in a by-now immortal letter to a snobbish country club that solicited his membership. See my heartfelt testimonial to Mr. Marx as a social critic, in my *People I Have Loved, Known, or Admired,* McGraw-Hill, New York, 1970, pp. 59–75.

121. My father said this at the end of a telephone call; for more about that lovely man see *Ibid.* pp. 21–33.

122. A threadbare witticism, but *I* laughed when I heard it.

123. This lump-in-the-throat acknowledgment, as delicious a malapropism as ever man uttered, was coined by Yogi Berra in a public ceremony on "Yogi Berra Day" in Sportsman's Park, the baseball field in St. Louis. Were I writing a gazette of American cities, I would identify St. Louis as, among other glories, "birthplace of Yogi Berra."

124. Some child said this, according to Art Linkletter; I say the kid is a genius.

125. Leo Rosten, positively adapted from *My Handy-dandy Plan to Save Our Colleges, op. cit.*

126. This is a duplicate of number 32. *Nu?*

127. From the Newark (Del.) *Weekly,* as reported in the *Reader's Digest,* God knows when.

128. Gregory Ratoff or Hamish Cooze, the pseudonym I have conferred on a famous confectioner.

129. You will find this in Norton Mockridge, *Fractured English;* it originally appeared in Mr. Mockridge's newspaper column; it is also reported in one of L. L. Levinson's dictionaries of acrobatic English.

130. H*Y*M*A*N K*A*P*L*A*N, in *The Education of* the man of the same name.

131. From a Four Marx Brothers Broadway musical comedy; the line was uttered by Groucho; whether it was original with him or was in the script, I do not know.

132. Linkletter, *A Child's Garden of Misinformation,* p. 31.

133. Anonymous, who also originated countless witticisms subsequently credited to subsequent utterers.

134. Leo Rosten, alas.

135. Ditto; that this pun has not been printed before, so far as I know, makes me respect the invisibility of the obvious.

136. I first heard this in Hollywood, *circa* 1940.

137. Some children say Achilles' mother held him by the heel and dipped him in the River Stynx.

138. Will wonders never cease? This gorgeous *gaffe* appeared in the Philadelphia (Pa.) *Bulletin,* according to the erudite Earle Tempel, *Press Boners.*

139. Leonard L. Levinson, *op. cit.*

140. Art Linketter, in a *Child's Garden of Misinformation,* quoting some child who deserves a Pulitzer Prize.

141. Leonard L. Levinson, *The Left Handed Dictionary,* p. 93.

142. H*Y*M*A*N K*A*P*L*A*N, *op. cit.;* this combines several of Mr. Kaplan's peculiar visions of American history.

143. Levinson, *op. cit.*

144. I first heard this at Crane Technical High School in Chicago and from delirious tourists in Rome, after that.

145. Leo Rosten.

146. H*Y*M*A*N K*A*P*L*A*N.

147. Author unknown, but believed to be Vayr Vayst.

148. Leo Rosten, who can't help it.

149. H*Y*M*A*N K*A*P*L*A*N.

150. Leo Rosten.

151. Leonard L. Levinson, I think.

152. *Ibid.* But this time, I'm sure: *The Left Handed Dictionary,* p. 188.

153. Evan Esar, *op. cit.*

154. Art Linkletter, *Kids Sure Rite Funny!*

155. Adapted from Levinson, *op. cit.,* p. 200.

156. Leo Rosten—and what a lovely cartoon Robert Day created for this one.

157. This *was* a real sign, carried in a parade in Dublin; reported to me by Professor Bergen Evans.

158. Leo Rosten, who is getting tired.

159. Adapted from Alban Norris, Sr., *How to Lip the Trite Fantastic,* Exposition Press, New York, 1959, p. 29. I don't know who Alban Norris, Jr., is.

160. I perpetrated this one.

183

161. I heard a policeman say this at 8:07 P.M., November 5, 1970, on the television program "To Tell the Truth." No one laughed, but I fell out of bed.

162. Leo Rosten, an unpaid commercial.

163. *Ibid.*

164. Evan Esar, *op. cit.,* p. 69.

165. Tujunga (Calif.) *Record-Ledger,* quoted by the invaluable Tempel, *Press Boners.*

166. This must go back to the nineteenth century; within the past year I have heard it credited, however, to Hamish Cooze (*op. cit.*), Yogi Berra, and a friend's wife's sister's mother-in-law.

167. Wellsboro (Pa.) *Gazette,* quoted by Earle Tempel.

168. Definitely *H*Y*M*A*N K*A*P*L*A*N,* in *The Return of H*Y*M*A*N K*A*P*L*A*N, op. cit.*

169. A Miami dowager, mother of a television *alrightnik.*

170. Adapted from *H*Y*M*A*N K*A*P*L*A*N,* by the writer thereof.

171. From *The Education of H*Y*M*A*N K*A*P*L*A*N.*

172. Adapted from Art Linkletter, *A Child's Garden of Misinformation.*

173. Ditto.

174. Ditto.

175. Leonard L. Levinson, no doubt.

176. Leo Rosten, likewise.

177. Levinson, *Left Handed Dictionary,* p. 65.

178. Told to me by Maurice Samuel, an elegant and perceptive writer.

179. Linkletter, *Kids Sure Rite Funny!*

180. Alban Norris, Sr., *op. cit.,* p. 22.

181. Some contestant on a television panel show. So sue me.

182. Yogi Berra, says Art Linkletter. Alas, poor Yogi.

183. Robert Day went out and committed this crack all by himself—or, at least, supplied the cartoon with no help whatsoever from me.

184

184. This is my rewrite and condensation of a story in Evan Esar's *Humorous English, op. cit.*

185. Yogi Berra, again quoted by Linkletter, *I Wish I'd Said That* (I do, too), Doubleday, 1968; or was it in *Kids Sure Rite Funny!?*

186. This, perhaps the most famous of all the glittering malapropisms assigned to Samuel Goldwyn, should be treated with caution, as I suggested, with evidence, in the introduction to this chrestomathy: "The Mischief of Language."

187. *The Education of H°Y°M°A°N K°A°P°L°A°N,* p. 11.

188. Linkletter, *A Child's Garden of Misinformation,* p. 32.

189. Evan Esar, *op. cit.,* p. 120.

190. Jerome ("Dizzy") Dean, superlative pitcher for the St. Louis Cardinals and the Chicago Cubs, later a sports newscaster of equal virtuosity.

191. In the New York *Herald Tribune,* as culled by that indefatigable culler, Earle Tempel, *Press Boners.*

192. The great Goldwyn.

193. Earle Tempel, *More Press Boners.*

194. *Ibid.*

195. St. Louis *Globe-Democrat,* as quoted in Earle Tempel, *Press Boners,* p. 16. Thank you, thank you, Mr. Tempel.

196. This priceless doggerel has tickled my fancy since the day I heard it recited with great solemnity by a dean of the Wharton School of Business, University of Pennsylvania. I never studied there.

197. Steve Lawrence, the night-club troubadour, who must have an excellent gag writer.

198. Mr. Hyman Kaplan, in his unnerving rendition of the most famous speech in Macbeth; see *The Education of H°Y°M°A°N K°A°P°L°A°N,* p. 108.

199. *Ibid.,* but a different story, unrelated to Shakespeare, who was unrelated to Mr. Kaplan.

200. This devastating wisecrack, made outside a funeral service in Beverly Hills for one of Hollywood's most disliked

producers, was promptly attributed to Red Skelton/George Jessel.

201. Ditto.

202. I hesitate to say who originated this, but I'm sure it has laid many a convention of CPAs in the aisles. CPAs are not accustomed to rolling in aisles.

203. In an indignant letter to me, from a reader protesting my analysis of some weighty problem.

204. Elgin (Ill.) *Courier-News,* quoted by Earle Tempel, naturally, in *Press Boners.*

205. H*Y*M*A*N K*A*P*L*A*N, in *The Education* thereof, p. 24.

206. New York *Journal American,* quoted by Irreplaceable Tempel, *Press Boners.*

207. Don Herold, who made many a memorable remark.

208. I shall never forget this one, from Linkletter's *Kids Sure Rite Funny!*

209. A neighbor of mine in Springdale, Conn. (when I was living in Springdale, Conn.) told me that her son had written this monstrous note to her neighbor's daughter. Hell lies about us in our infancy.

210. Jean Cocteau.

211. Groucho Marx, quoted in my dissertation, *People I have Loved, Known or Admired,* p. 60.

212. Happily reported, about himself, by Mr. Okum, when he was appointed to the President's Council of Economic Advisors.

213. A movie agent in New York, who clearly loved his wife—while she was in London.

214. This must have come from the same agent.

215. From the New York *Times,* as quoted by Earle Tempel, *Press Boners.*

216. Art Linkletter, *A Child's Garden of Misinformation,* p. 48—simple, clear, indisputable and delicious.

217. Mansfield (Ohio) *Tribune,* I think, in Earle Tempel (again?!), *Press Boners.*

218. Linkletter, A *Child's Garden of Misinformation*—and how I wish I had said it.

219. Adapted from *Ibid.*

220. The author of the book in your eager little hands.

221. The witty, oft-neglected newspaper columnist Frank ("Kin") Hubbard, a source of many epigrams.

222. Norton Mockridge, *op. cit.*, p. 22.

223. Abraham Beame, when running as a candidate for Mayor of New York. I didn't believe it, either. Mr. Beame lost.

224. Norton Mockridge, *op. cit.*, p. 34.

225. Heaven only knows who first said this, or first stole it, or first did a double-take about it.

226. An English politician, campaigning in the Midlands, during a heated borough campaign. (Heated boroughs are more comfortable than cold ones.)

226A. A cynical, clinical psychiatrist—about scrutable, experimental psychologists.

227. I would like to credit the psychologist who got off this nifty observation, but the social scientists I have queried merely wince.

228. Henry Morgan—the comedian, not the pirate; the two categories are not always resolutely separated.

229. Reported to me by Richard Manoff, a dandy fellow.

230. Samuel Goldwyn, to whom I genuflect.

231. A commercial for a breakfast food, on a California radio program.

232. A radio announcer, unknown by name, which must be welcome news to him.

233. An inadvertence by the late Dorothy Kilgallen, during an animated discussion on television.

234. Vic Marsillo, a manager of pugilists, in a radio interview, as quoted by John Lardner in *The New Yorker*, June 6, 1959, p. 158.

235. An announcer on an Oakland (Calif.) radio station. See note 232.

236. Dave Garroway, a most literate and thoughtful gentleman, while delivering a commercial for a Swiss watch on the NBC-TV "Today Show." It could have happened to anyone.

237. This is one of the most famous boners heard on American radio; it was enshrined in a phonograph record, years ago, called "Bloopers." Some *gonif* never returned my platter.

238. An announcer, allegedly, on WABC, New York—and I'm grateful to him.

239. Linkletter, *A Child's Garden of Misinformation,* p. 18.

240. Alban Norris, Sr., *op. cit.,* p. 37.

241. Little ole me.

242. Ditto.

243. If not Samuel Goldwyn, then who?

244. Indubitably Mr. Goldwyn, as reported to me by his host, who owned the sun-dial.

245. Anonymous, the most modest man in any anthology.

246. A cab driver, to me, with complete *savoir faire,* the day after the second landing on the moon; at the stop light at 54th Street and Second Avenue.

247. Anonymous.

248. Linkletter, *A Child's Garden of Misinformation.*

249. Adapted from *Kids Sure Rite Funny!*

250. A journal in Owensburg (Kans.). The visual reconstruction haunts me. Quoted by (sigh!) Earle Tempel, in *Press Boners.* I have not been able to find Owensburg in Kansas.

251. Charles Dillon ("Casey") Stengel, in analyzing for sports reporters how the glorious New York Mets made such a meteoric dash for the baseball championship of the world.

252. Dizzy Dean, on one of his radio programs. Mr. Dean should be drafted back to the air waves—despite the objection of teachers of English.

253. Evan Esar, *op. cit.,* p. 121.

254. I heard this a dozen times during various world series contests held in Manhattan.

255. I see no way to avoid hanging this one on Mr.

Goldwyn; it was told to me by a man of unimpeachable reliability.

256. Blame me for this one.

257. Easton (Pa.) *Express,* quoted by Earle Tempel, *Press Boners.*

258. From *The Joys of Yiddish, op. cit.*

259. A radio announcer whose fame spread like wildfire, but whose name vanished in the protective mist of history.

260. A fledging weather forecaster, according to Art Linkletter.

261. A Minneapolis radio announcer, quoted by Will Jones in the Minneapolis *Tribune.*

262. I first heard this attributed to Alexander Woollcott, but he may have been quoting someone else, who was quoting a weather forecaster or newspaper columnist in the Midwest; the remark has also been credited to "F.P.A." (Franklin P. Adams), Heywood Broun and Fred Allen. Whenever a list includes the name of Fred Allen, I put my money on him.

Postscript: My thanks go out to all those rare souls, young and old, culprits or collectors, who made this book necessary.

—*Leo Rosten*

ABOUT THE AUTHOR (sort of)

Leo Rosten, author of *Hamlet* and other best sellers, is a former native of Chicago. Many readers ask, "How does he write with such a rare combination of wit and wisdom?" That is a good question.

Mr. Rosten is one of the world's leading authorities on metallurgy. When the Pentagon discovered that he was allergic to metal, they told him he could best contribute to the American war effort by joining the Luftwaffe.

It is not generally known that Mr. Rosten is a prolific inventor. Among his inventions are the knuckle (today, some people use as many as twenty-eight knuckles on their hands alone) and antimony, which has made inflation fashionable.

Mr. Rosten lives in an abandoned rut in Coxsackie, New York, where he spends many a happy hour on his hobbies: a collection of pores, which he inherited, and a colligation of boomerangs, which he cannot seem to get rid of.

An inveterate traveler, he has carried a small hollow pipe with him on his journeys ever since he learned, in Manhattan, that the surest way to get heat is by banging on a pipe.

Mr. Rosten's next opus will be an index to the dictionary.